# UNLEASHING

# Your

# PURPOSE

## *DISCOVER YOURE UNIQUE SIGNIFICANCE*

# CLIFTON CLARKE

The book was printed in the United States of America

ISBN 978-1-943844-49-4


Published by Global Empowerment Network Press

To contact the author, please write to:

1317 E. Little Creek Road

Norfolk

VA 23452


Or Email: drcliftonclarke@gmail.com

# CONTENTS

# DEDICATION

To

JOEL

# Acknowledgments

I am forever grateful to Almighty God with whom I have walked with for thirty-four years. I have given you the prime years of my life and You have given me purpose, meaning and significance in return.

I am deeply grateful to my wife Marcia and my two children Joel and Jessica for their continued love and laughter. I owe a great debt of gratitude to my mother Hilda Clarke for her encouragement and prayers.

A special thank you to my sister Maureen. You have always challenged me to climb higher and pushed me to go further.

Thanks to all my students at Regent University for giving me the privilege to be their professor and teacher.

Last but by no means least, thanks to my Restoration Christian Fellowship family for allowing me to be your pastor and spiritual leader.

# Unleashing Your Purpose
## By Dr. Clifton Clarke

# CHAPTER 1: INTRODUCTION

*Without a purpose, life is motion without meaning, activity without direction, and events without reason. Without a purpose, life is trivial, petty, and pointless.*
RICK WARREN

Have you ever wondered why you were born? Was it just an accident of nature or could it be that you were born for a reason?  Have you ever pondered these questions? Have you ever wondered what you're supposed to accomplish here—what kind of a legacy you're meant to leave behind? The purpose of this book is to help you discover the answer to those important but often-haunting questions.

We all search for significance; we want our lives to matter, to mean something. When life is over and our time on earth is up we want to know that it counted for something important. Thankfully each of us has been given different gifts, talents and skills that we're meant to use for the good of others and to make the world a better place.

Studies have shown that when we use our talents to benefit others our lives take on much greater meaning and we are ultimately far happier than if we had lived only for self-gratification. And living a life of meaning comes a sense of significance. Fulfilling our purpose is our reason for being.  It's why we're here on this earth and the reason we get out of bed every morning. The hopeful truth is that each of us has a unique purpose for living. It's up to us to discover that purpose and fulfill it.

Unfortunately, discovering our purpose for living is not wary. The answer depends on how we answer other basic questions such as:

What does it mean to have purpose? What do we base it on—what source is reliable enough to consult for such a life-changing discovery? There are no easy answers to these questions, but we can find wisdom from others who have made it their life's work to discover the answers. In his book, *The Power of Purpose*, Author Richard Leider made this profound statement:

> Purpose is fundamental to human life. It is what makes us human. Purpose is not only what makes us human, it is the one thing that cannot be taken from us. Purpose gives us the will to live or to persevere. It gives us a reason to get up in the morning. Purpose gives us courage.[1]

Each of us want our lives to matter, and we want to live courageously. Purpose is one of the chief requisites for courage. One constant in the lives of people who experience a sense of courage is the 'purpose moment'—that moment of meaning.[2] Moses saw an Egyptian beating a Hebrew slave and decided to intervene, (see Ex. 2:11); German reformer Martin Luther nailed the

---

[1] Richard Leider, *The Power of Purpose* (San Francisco, CA: Barrett-Koehler Publishers, 2010), 3
[2] Ibid.

Ninety-Five Theses to the door of the prestigious All Saints Church in Wittenberg, questioning the Catholic Church's practice of selling indulgences taking exception to the notion of a papal pardon rather than penance or genuine contrition; Rosa Parks decided not to give up her seat to a white passenger in the segregated South; Nelson Mandela refused to sign a conditional re

lease from prison to renounce violence against the evil apartheid regime. Few of our purpose moments will be that dramatic but each one is just as meaningful. The purpose moment is when our passion, purpose and destiny flash before us in one single action or thought. My purpose here is to help you to find and recognize that 'purpose moment' in order to discover your own particular life's significance.

The Bible is a book about the purpose and

meaning of human significance. According to Holy Scripture, our purpose—the ultimate reason we're here—is to glorify God. In other words, as those created in His image, our purpose is to praise God, worship Him, to proclaim His greatness, and to accomplish His will in all that we do and all that we are. In the process of glorifying God, we find our reason to live. We were created by Him, according to His grand design and plan; and we are here to accomplish what He has for us to do. When we trust the one who has made us, who works all things after the counsel of His will (Eph. 1:11), then we are able to live a life of purpose and passion. How the particulars of that purpose are expressed, however, is up to us.

*L*et's begin by defining what we mean by purpose. The word "purpose," translated from Hebrew, means "original intent" or "reason for creation." According to Steve Lambert, purpose is one of five elements of vision. Lambert asserts that purpose is the *driving force* of *vision*. Purpose is what *defines* and *drives* the vision home. Of all the elements of *vision*, purpose is the most critical because without it there will be no meaning to the vision. Without a place to go—a *destination* or *destiny*—there's no need for a *vehicle*. Without destiny there is no need for purpose.[3] Purpose then, is the substance of destiny.

---

[3] Steven Lambert, *Prophetic Purpose*. Online article located at http://www.slm.org/prophetc/articles/prophetic_purpose1.pdf

Purpose and destiny are not *synonymous*, but are *synergistic*. They are inextricably linked and codependent, yet distinct. One is meaningless without the other. Purpose has no reason to exist without destiny, for purpose is the servant of destiny. Indeed destiny cannot be attained without purpose. The late Myles Munroe taught us much about purpose and potential. In his book *In Pursuit of Purpose*, he explained:

> Everything in life has a purpose. Everyone on this planet was born with and for a purpose. It is this purpose that is the only source of meaning. Without purpose, life is an experiment or a haphazard journey that results in frustration, disappointment and failure. Without purpose, life is subjective, or it is a trial and error game that is ruled by environmental influences and the circumstances of the moment. Likewise, in the absence of purpose, time has no meaning, energy has no reason and life has no precision. Therefore, it is essential that we understand and discover our purpose in life so that we can experience an

effective, full and rewarding life.[4]

Purpose, he continued, is:

> ...the original intent for the creation of a thing,

> ...the original reason for the existence of a thing,

> ...the end for which the means exist,

> ...the cause for the creation of a thing,

> ...the desired result that initiates production,

> ...the need that makes a manufacturer produce a specific product,

> ...the destination that prompts the journey,

> ...the expectation of the source,

> ...the objective for the subject,

> ...the aspiration for the inspiration, and

[4] Myles Munroe, *In Pursuit of Purpose* (Shippenburg, PA: Destiny Image, 1992), 6

...the object one wills or resolves to have.[5]

---

**Every product is the child of purpose.**

---

Purpose, therefore, is the original intent in the mind of the creator that motivated him to create a particular item. That also explains the reason for its existence. Every product is a child of purpose. In other words, before any product is made, there is a purpose established in the mind of the manufacturer that gives conception to the idea that becomes the substance for the design and production of the product. Thus, purpose precedes production.

Recently, a study, entitled, 'Discovering What Matters', explored the way people prioritize their lives as they face challenges. It revealed that regardless of age, gender, financial status or life phase, the majority of people with a sense of purpose in their lives were more likely to report being "happy" and to describe themselves as living the "good life." Having a sense of purpose

---

[5] Ibid., 7

was related to possessing both a "focus" on essential things today, and a "vision" of the future they wanted to enjoy.

*E*veryone is born with a one-of-a-kind personal destiny. In order to attain unto that destiny, we must have a *vision* of our destiny. Envisioning knowing our destiny acts as a road map to tell us where we're going, and our purpose takes us there. As someone has so aptly said, "If you don't know where you're going, any road will get you there." That's why God told the prophet Habakkuk to write the *vision* down— to delineate it, explain it, make it plain, make it understandable—so that those who are running to complete the vision, those who are running in the race, may run toward the finish line without getting off track or lost. You can't run to the finish line, or kick the ball into the goal, if you don't know where they are.

### God's Divine Purpose

> This is the plan determined for the whole world; his is the hand stretched out over all nations. For the LORD Almighty has

purposed, and who can thwart him? His hand is stretched out, and who can turn it back? (Isa. 14:26-27)

Also

> This is the plan determined for the whole world; this is the hand stretched out over all nations. For the Lord Almighty has purposed, and who can thwart him? His hand is stretched out, and who can turn it back? (Eph 1:11)

It seems clear from the teaching of Scripture that all events of nations and individuals are known to God from the beginning and that they are taken into account in His plan and purpose. This does not mean that God causes and is responsible for all acts and events, but that they are part of His purpose in the sense that He works all thing to His ultimate glory.[6]

---

[6] Guy Duffied and Nathaniel Cleave, *Foundation of Pentecostal Theology* (Los Angeles, CA: Four Square Media, 2006), 81.

## *Jesus' Primary Purpose*

To understand the true meaning of living on purpose, we must turn to the prophetic proto-type Who exemplified a life of purpose, Jesus Christ Himself and examine carefully the meaning and purpose inherent in his earthly life and ministry. John the beloved disciple declared:

> "The Son of God appeared for this purpose, that He might destroy the works of the devil." (1 John 3:8)

This passage makes it clear that Jesus had a purpose and mission on earth, which was ultimately to destroy, negate, undo, reverse and bring to naught the works of the devil through God's redemptive plan. The end goal in walking in God's purpose was the restoration and redemption of God's creational order that was corrupted, perverted and distorted by the devil. Jesus had a mission, a calling and a destiny. It was His purpose that drove Him to the cross in spite of the suffering (see Is. 53). When Jesus prayed for the Father to take the cup of suffering from Him, He was not using rhetorical hyperbole (see Luke

22:42). It was because He was focused on His calling, purpose and mission that propelled Him toward a cruel death. His destiny was to fulfill the Father's will and to destroy the works of the devil. Jesus had a purpose that was tied to His destiny and so do we. It was for the joy that was set before Him that He endured the cross—the sheer euphoria of foreseeing mankind at last redeemed by the blood of the lamb, and restored to right standing and relationship with Father God! This final outcome—redemption and restoration—is what motivated the God of Love and "the God of all Grace" (1 Peter 5:10) to come to earth and become one of us in order to give HIS life as a propitiation, a substitutionary sacrifice, in exchange for ours!

After Jesus arose from the dead and just prior to ascending back to His Father, He instructed His disciples to also 'be about the Father's business'—to 'occupy until He returns' (Luke 19:13). Today Jesus' instructions apply to us as disciples as well. We do this by listening to His voice and performing the works of Jesus, doing the things that He did during His earthly ministry. All genuine ministry is merely the extension of the ministry and mission of Jesus.

$J$ust before His Day of Ascension, an amazing transaction took place in the realm of the Spirit, which then many believers did not fully grasp any more than we do today. The apostle Paul put it like this:

> *"Therefore it says, when He ascended on High, He led captive a host of captives, and He gave gifts to men,"* (Now this expression, 'He ascended,' what does it mean except that He also had descended into the lower parts of the earth? He who descended is Him-self also He who ascended far above all the heavens, that He might fill all things.) And He gave some as apostles, and some as prophets, and some as evangelists, and some as pastors and teachers (Eph. 4:8-11).

This passage is one beloved by those of us in the Pentecostal, Charismatic and Renewal ministries. It affirms that when Jesus ascended to heaven He delegated to His people the ministry giftings He Himself had manifested during His earthly ministry. The giftings that He imparted were what we now refer to as the "Fivefold Ministry Offices." (See Eph. 4:11.) As you continue reading you will begin to realize that your purpose is related to the gifts given to you by the Holy Spirit.

# Chapter 2

## IN PURSUIT OF PURPOSE

### Jeremiah 29:11

*For I know the plans I have for you, declares the Lord, plans for welfare and not for evil, to give you a future and a hope.*

The question I hear most often is *why*?

The adverb 'why' means, *for what purpose, reason, or cause; or with what intention, justification, or motive has such an event occurred?* The most commonly asked question is "Why was I born and for what purpose did I come into the world? We've all asked ourselves those questions at one time or another. The apostle Paul expressed his quest for purpose this way:

> Not that I have already obtained all this, or have already arrived at my goal, but I press on to take hold of that for which Christ Jesus took hold of me (Phil. 3:12).

Underlying this question is the quest for *meaning*. Is there a true meaning to life or are we trapped in a meaningless, purposeless universe of senseless acts and random occurrences? The fact that we come back time and time again to the question of purpose is clear evidence that we were not built to live in ignorance on this subject.

This quest for human meaning is poignantly seen in the writings of human philosophers who try to address the subject of purpose vs. purposelessness.

**Man-made answers to the question of meaning and purpose:**

Whether we are aware of it or not, many writings of ancient philosophies provide the basis of what our culture believes today. For instance, a British man by the name of Jeremy Bentham (1748-1832) taught what's known as Utilitarianism, where he defined the meaning of life as the greatest happiness principle. He believed that "nature has placed mankind under the governance of two sovereign masters, pain and pleasure." So by his estimation good is whatever brings the greatest happiness to the largest number of people. It can be summed up by a phrase you've no doubt heard people say: "Well, if it feels good and does not cause pain to others then it must be good, right?"

*N*ihilism is a philosophy touted by Greek philosopher Friedrich Nietzsche (485 BCE-380 BCE), who characterized nihilism this way: there are no moral absolutes except those contrived by man. To put it succinctly, nihilism is the process of "the devaluing of the highest values," saying that "God is dead," and as such, there are no moral rules by which man is required to live. His work is responsible for the moral relativism that is prominently seen today. It says that meaning and purpose is whatever we want it to be. In other words, truth is relative and purpose is subjective. We are to live by whatever we want to believe. Sound familiar?

*J*ohn-Paul Sartre (1905-1980) is the man responsible for what is known as *Existentialism.* This is very similar to nihilism, proposing that human beings create the meaning for their own lives. It goes on to say that meaning is not determined by a supernatural being or earthly authority, but each individual is free to determine his own meanings free from externally-imposed constraints.

*S*ecular humanism* is a widely-held philosophy of our day that rose from such a belief system. Secular humanism suggests that human beings are capable of being ethical and moral apart from religion or a God. In other words, individuals determine their purpose without supernatural influence; the human personality (in a general sense) determines the purpose of someone's life. This is basically a way of looking at the world that is entirely devoid of a supreme being, with the central focus on human beings. Wow, imagine a world left to the basic instincts of human nature without constraints of any kind.

*P*ostmodernism is the last of the basic philosophies used to define meaning and purpose in the world. In essence, postmodernism touts new ways of thinking, contrary to the original form. It is also known as deconstructionism, a kind of tearing down of fundamental beliefs, replaced by experiences that lead to understanding its own personal reality. Postmodernism is therefore skeptical of explanations that claim to be valid for all groups, cultures, traditions, or races, and instead focuses on the relative truths of each person or within each paradigm, that result in a relative view of reality. Postmodernism postulates that many, if not all, apparent realities are only social constructs and are therefore subject to change. It claims that there is no absolute truth and that the way people perceive the world is subjective and emphasizes the role of language, power relations, and motivations in the formation of ideas and beliefs. This belief system tends to govern popular opinion, particularly in the media.

**W**ell, I hope I haven't lost you through
the use of these fancy philosophical terms, because they play a vital role in this discussion.
There is one glaring basic fact we can't ignore if
we truly seek truth: *Human quest for purpose
and meaning is a hopeless endeavor apart from
God.*

Nothing in the created order carries meaning
within it, whether it is a tree or a car. The creator
is the only one who can unlock the meaning behind his design.
For our ultimate identity we are dependent on a
transcendent, the divine Creator. When viewed
theologically it signifies our fundamental *crea-
tureliness.* In this way the modern concept return
us to the traditional theological affirmation of
God as the origin of humankind. It also takes us
back to the conclusion that humans are God's
creatures. Because we are dependent on a transcendent reality, the ultimate origin of humankind
lies beyond the world. Stated theological our

origin is in God.[7] Paul makes this point in his speech to the Athenians when he quotes from an ancient Greek poet, *"For in him we live and move and have our being,* (Acts 17: 28). Although many Christians apply one or more of these philosophies to their personal lives, I recommend that we explore what the Bible says about purpose and destiny, to set the scene for finding our special place there.

## A Biblical Response

The Bible was given to us as a blueprint to follow, allowing us to discover the purpose and meaning behind human existence. Yes, it does address factual issues such as the order of creation and matters of science, but essentially the Bible is a theological book inspired by God to make sense of the world and our place in it.

---

[7] Stanley J. Grenz, *Theology for the Community of God* (Grand Rapids, Michigan: William B. Eerdman's Publishing Company, 1994), 139.

Below are five basic biblical truths that lay the foundations for our journey toward discovering God's purpose for our lives:

1. **Meaning and purpose cannot be found within this world alone**

Without God, life has no purpose, and without purpose, life has no meaning. Without meaning, life has no significance or hope.

The writer of Ecclesiastes says in Chapter 1, verses 2-3:

> The words of the Preacher, the son of David, king in Jerusalem.
> "Vanity of vanities," says the Preacher;
> "Vanity of vanities, all is vanity."
> What profit has a man from all his labor
> In which he toils under the sun?

Surrounded by more success, opulence, and pleasure than any person could ever desire, Solomon hit rock bottom in deep misery having failed in his search for meaning through wealth, power and possessions. He began by frankly admitting his emptiness and inability to help himself. Solomon confessed that his view of life was bleak and hopeless with nothing to live for apart from God. We too must come to the same conclusion before we can finally open our hearts, willing to let God show us His intentions for our divine purpose. Job 28:13 says, "Man does not comprehend its worth; it cannot be found in the land of the living." To put it another way, humankind does not know the real value of 'divine purpose,' because it cannot see with the eyes of heaven until it submits to God as Creator. Indeed the value of something is determined by its purpose, so that its value is greatly diminished apart from that knowledge. C. S. Lewis notes:

> If the whole universe has no meaning, we should never have found out that it has no meaning: just as, if there were no light in the universe and therefore no creatures with eyes, we should never know it was dark. Dark would be without meaning. — C.S. Lewis, *Mere Christianity*

## 2. We live in a fallen and sinful world

**W**e live in a fallen world. As a result of sin, the world has to contend with sickness, sorrow, evil and death. Everyone born into this world has the sin nature already dwelling inside them as a direct result of Adam's rebellion. Therefore, none of us is born truly innocent and pure, but we all have the innate tendency toward sin, desiring to be in control of our own lives, doing our own thing. Sin and evil are a reality in our world.

Romans 6:23 says this:

> For the wages of sin is death, but the gift of God is eternal life in Christ Jesus our Lord.

But what is sin? At this point we need to define certain terms. The two most popular definitions of sin are 'missing the mark' and 'transgression of the law'. Missing the mark means 'falling short of a predetermined goal in ignorance. *Transgression* also includes 'rebellion', or intentionally doing something in defiance of a rule or law. As long as we are in these physical bodies we will never be completely free from the influence of sin, but we cling to the promise that Christ will always be with us and that we can overcome sin and temptation by the power of the Holy Spirit that dwells within us.

In Matthew 28:20, Jesus said,
> "Lo I am with you always even to the end of the age." In John 17:15-16, we read, "I do not pray that You should take them out of the world, but that You should keep them from the evil one."

Robert G. Lee notes,
> Sin has ruined men and women. Sin has occasioned every tear of sorrow, every sigh of grief, every pang of agony. Sin has withered everything that is fair, blasted everything that is good, made better every that is sweet, dried up prings of comfort, rolled far and wide tides of sorrow. Sin has dug every grave, built every coffin,

woven every shroud, enlarged every cemetery….that the world has ever seen. [8]

The remarkable truth is that even though sin has power in this world it does not have power over you unless you yield to it and allow it to have free reign over you. And if you have made Jesus your Lord, receiving His salvation, the Holy Spirit lives inside you, empowering you to resist sin, and be victorious as you yield yourself to Him.

### 3.  We have Free will

Probably the most common definition of free will is the "ability to make choices without any prior prejudice, inclination, or disposition."

> *God created things which had free will. That means creatures which can go wrong or right. Some people think they can imagine a creature which was free but had no possibility of going wrong, but I can't. If a thing is free to be good it's also free to be bad. And free will is what has made evil possible. Why, then, did God give them free*

---

[8] Robert G. Lee, *Heart to Heart* (Nashville: Broadman Press, 1977), 65-66.

*will? Because free will, though it
makes evil possible, is also the only
thing that makes possible any love or
goodness or joy worth having.*[9]

Proverb 19:9 tells us:
In their hearts humans plan their course, but the
LORD establishes their steps."

Joshua 24:15 says this:
But if serving the LORD seems undesira-
ble to you, then choose for yourselves this
day whom you will serve, whether the
gods your forefathers served beyond the
River, or the gods of the Amorites, in
whose land you are living. But as for me
and my household, we will serve the
LORD.

With the freedom to choose love and beauty also
comes the freedom to choose evil and wicked-
ness.

---

[9] C. S. Lewis, *Mere Christianity*, 89

## 4.  There will be a day of reckoning

Real believers understand that there is far
more to life than just the few years we live on
this planet. Human lives are but a short and
quiet blip on the radar of time, but according to
God's Word physical death is not the end of
existence. Every person ever born will live forever in eternity, either in heaven or hell. J. I.
Packer notes, "There are few things stressed
more strongly in the Bible than the reality of
God's work as Judge." [10] "The vague and ten-
uous hope that God is too kind to punish the
ungodly has become a deadly opiate for the
consciences of millions. It hushes their fears
and allows them to practice all pleasant forms
of iniquity while death draws everyday
nearer and the command to repent goes un-
heeded," says A. W. Tozer.[11]

The Christian should remain acutely
aware of his *temporary assignment* on earth
so that his lifestyle, values and decisions will
reflect the glory of God in all he says and

---

[10] *J. I. Packer, Knowing God (Downers Grove, IL: Inter Varsity, 1973, 125.*
[11] *A. W. Tozer, The Knowledge of the Holy (New York: Harper & Row, Publishers, 1961), 95.*

does. In the end, our true identity is established in eternity and heaven is our ultimate homeland. Philip Yancy, writing in Christianity Today, noted that although 71 percent of American believe in an afterlife, no one talks about it much. "Percentages don't apply to eternity, of course; but for the sake of argument, assume that 99 percent of our existence will take place in heaven. Isn't it a little bizarre that we simply ignore heaven, acting as if it doesn't matter. [12] If our response to the gospel is foreordained in the sense that god determined it for no reason except his own mysterious, sovereign will, then "free choice" is a mirage.[13]

Hebrews 9:27 tells us:
> Just as man is destined to die once, and after that to face judgment.

Bonhoeffer maintained that there are five different deaths every Christian should die:

---

[12] *Philip Yancy, Heaven Can't Wait, "Christianity Today, September 7, 1984, 53.*
[13] *Grenz, 452.*

1. Death to Natural Relationship. It is one thing for husband for husband or a father to be persecuted, it is quite another to see children suffer a similar fate. Hitler always used a man's family as an inducement for absolute obedience. Bonhoeffer held the conviction that our commitment to Christ should be so all-compassing that all natural affection must come under its authority (Matt 10:37).
2. Death to success. Bonhoeffer said, "Success is a veneer that covers only the emptiness of the soul."
3. Death to the flesh. The Christian should have no fear of suffering, for he is already dead to self.
4. Death to the love of money.
5. Physical death for Christ, should a person be thus called.[14]

The unchangeable truth is that there will

ultimately be a day of reckoning.

---

[14] Erwin W. Lutzer, *Hitler's Cross* (Chicago: Moody Press, 1995), 182 – 186.

God has ordained three inalterable appointments for each of us: an appointed death, an appointed judgment and an appointed Savior.

The decrees and mandates of God are certain and inevitable, whether we want to believe it or not. On the other side of death, no man will be able to argue with reality, though he may have fought it to his last breath. Once we as Christians reach heaven, our purpose on earth will clearly be revealed, but we dare not miss it while on earth, because once we get to heaven it will be too late to make any difference.

## 5.  This world is not our final resting place

Just as life on earth are both a *test* and a *trial*, the Bible uses various metaphors and blunt scripture verses to make it clear that life on this earth is a *temporary assignment*—that (1) it is extremely brief when compared with eternity and (2) the planet on which we live is merely a *temporary residence*. Each person is only on earth for a visit; it will not be that person's final destination. With that fact firmly settled in our minds, we should all live with eternity's values in view, focusing on living to love and obey Him until He comes again or takes us home in death. In fact, anyone who comes to this understanding will find that his outlook, values and lifestyle have been truly transformed. Revelation 21:1-3 details the final destination for those that belong to Jesus:

> "Then I saw a new heaven and a new earth, for the first heaven and the first earth had passed away, and there was no longer any sea. I saw the Holy City, the New Jerusalem, coming down out of heaven from God, prepared as a bride beautifully dressed for her husband. And I heard a loud voice from the throne saying, "Now the dwelling of God is with men, and he will live with them. They will be his people, and God himself will be with them and be their God."

Earth is but a pilgrim's stay, a pilgrim's journey, a pilgrim's tent. Heaven is a city, permanent, God-planned, whose foundations are as stable as God's throne," observes E. M. Bounds.[15] If you

---

[15] E. M. Bound, Heaven: A Place, A City, A Home (Grand Rapids, MI: Baker Books House, 1975), 13.

read history you will find that the Christians who did most for the present world were precisely those who thought most of the next, say C.S Lewis.[16] Lewis further admonishes, "Aim at Heaven and you will get earth "thrown in": aim at earth and your will get neither.[17]

When we get to heaven we want to be able to

say, "I have accomplished the purpose for which you called me into this world."

---

[16] C. S. Lewis, Mere Christianity, springs in the Valley (Los Angeles: Cowman Publications, Inc., 1939), 238.
[17] Ibid. 104.

# Chapter 3
# PLANTED AND POSITIONED ON PURPOSE

**Isaiah 61:3**

*They will be called oaks of righteousness, a planting of the LORD for the display of his splendor*

The key to knowing our purpose lies in knowing God—having a personal relationship with Him. Only through relationship can we discover our purpose. Put simply there is no purpose outside of relationship with God. Unless God reveals your assignment and you align with His will, you will never be fulfilled or completely satisfied with even your crowning achievements. Your purpose is not some abstract notion that's floating just out of reach, and that you will never grasp. Once we have a relationship with God we can ask Him to clarify and make plain exactly the direction we are supposed to take. When we ask, He promises to answer, revealing our very destiny—the thing that will bring us more joy than we can even imagine. Why do you think God has invested so much in keeping open the lines of communication with Him? It's because apart from relationship with Him our lives have absolutely no real meaning. Even when we were dead (see Ephesians 2) God did not give up on us but quickened us and made us born again–why? Because He values relationship with us. God values relationship with us because that is the only way He can communicate to us our *raison d'etre* (reason for being). In this chapter we're going to look at the importance of being positioned according to and in line with our purpose.

## Purpose and Positioning

It's vital that we position ourselves to discover

our purpose. If indeed our lives are to have purpose, how do we position ourselves to live and walk according to that purpose? Let me illustrate this process using the growth cycle of a seed.

In 1 Peter 1:23 we read:

> For you have been born again, not of perishable seed, but of imperishable [seed], through the living and enduring word of God.

Did you know that you are a seed? Well, let me assure you that you're a seed planted by God. Listen to what Isaiah 61:3 says:

> They will be called oaks of righteousness, a planting of the LORD for the display of his splendor.

You and I (and in another sense, our potential) are seeds planted in the world by God and our purpose is to bring forth fruit for His glory (Gen

1:26-28). God in His wisdom created land and sowed all types of seeds into it. One particular seed that was precious to Him was *man*. Adam was planted in the best possible environment to ensure his survival. From this we can see that *location* is vital to our success. As long as Adam was in Eden he was successful. As soon as he sinned and was expelled from Eden, Adam lost control of the land and the forces of nature. From then on man would not have a natural tendency toward God but toward living for himself, and thereby bowing to the will of the devil. From that point on, man worshiped all kinds of things in order to survive. Idolatry is therefore the natural religion of all natural ungodly men. But once we are in relationship with God, we are His seed and what He has spoken over us will ultimately come to pass. He has redeemed us back to Himself by sacrificing His only begotten Son. Notice something about the makeup of a seed (see figure 1 below).

Figure 1

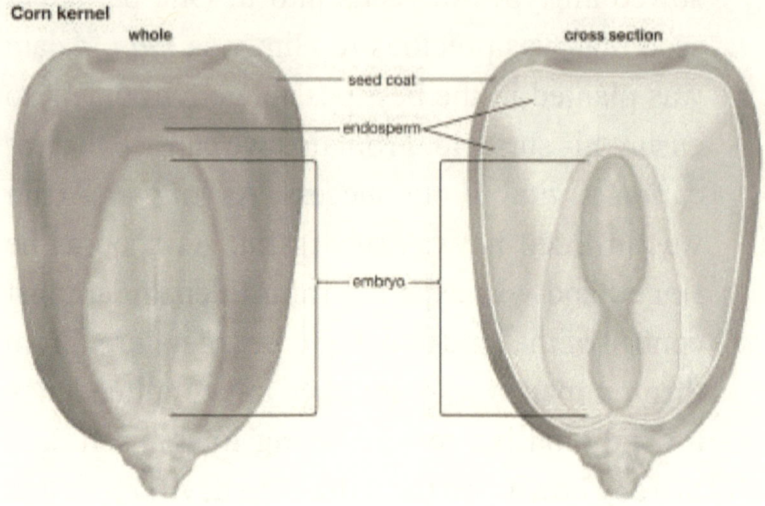



There is the outer coat (Body), known as the endosperm (that includes the soul with its emotions and intellect)–the seed coat that protects and feeds the embryo, and the embryo itself–the source of life (also known as the spirit). Below are listed important principles that will help us grasp the incredible truth, that we are God's seed. There we'll examine how this relates to discovering His purpose for our lives.

**A seed has to be planted in the ground within a certain time period or else the embryo will die.**

Within the lifetime of the seed there is a time limit for growth or else the seed will die. In the same way there is a sense of urgency in discovering our life's purpose as one planted by the Lord. Psalms 102:11 captures the fleeting nature of our lives:

> My days are like an evening shadow that stretches out and declines [with the sun]; and I am withered like grass (AMP).

Notice something about the seed once it is sown into the ground. The seed does not consult the soil for its purpose, rather its carries its own DNA. As God's seed you may be planted in very difficult situations. Therefore it's important for you to know that you get your identity from your Father in heaven and not from the soil in which you're planted. By soil I mean location, situation, circumstances where you are expected to thrive. You could be like Joseph and be placed in a pit to die, but because he refused to allow the pit to define him, he was made fit for the palace.

Observe also the intentionality of the planter. The Bible says God planted you (See Isa. 61:3). Even if it appears otherwise you must believe that everything in your life is intentional. You were not discarded or randomly thrown to the ground; rather you were planted. That means you weren't an afterthought; you did not just come to be. You were planted, God carefully placed you where you are and He is watching over your growth. Before God sent Jeremiah, the prophet out to face the stiff-necked, backslidden nation of Judah whose people were on the brink of exile, God reminded Jeremiah that he belonged to Him and that Jeremiah was created and called for His purpose:

> "Before I formed you in the womb I knew you;
> Before you were born I sanctified you;
> I ordained you a prophet to the nations"
> (Jer. 1:5 NKJV).

God knew you, just as he knew Jeremiah, long before you were born or even conceived. He thought about you and planned your future, with great delight, excited about the very day you were born. When you feel discouraged or inadequate, remember that God has always thought of you as valuable and that He has a purpose in mind for you. You are constantly on His mind.

**The seed has to position itself for death before life can emerge.**

In our diagram above (figure 1) the outer coat is just temporary. After the seed is protected and nurtured in the casein outer coating the outer shell begins to give way and the endosperm emerges. In other words the seed has to undergo a dying process before new life can emerge. The seed, therefore, uses the ground to align itself for death. Jesus was referring to this when he said in John 12:24:

> Most assuredly, I say to you, unless a grain of wheat falls into the ground and dies, it remains alone; but if it dies, it produces much grain.

In order to discover God's purpose for our lives, we have to die to our own purposes and design plans. Jesus is our example because He always chose to set aside His own plans in order to do the will of His Father.

> "Father, if you are willing, take this cup from me; yet not my will, but yours *be done."* *(Luke 22: 42, NKJ)*

---

You plant a seed for it to come back greater than when it entered the ground.

---

The individual who "dies to self" understands that God created him for a reason; that he is a part of God's plan for the world. To be used of God one must understand the "essence of who he now really is," and how it is that God can use him. Every genuine child of God wants to be used by God to accomplish His purposes in the world — Jesus said, "By this My Father is glorified, that you bear much fruit, and so prove to be My disciples"(Jn 15:8). That is the essence of God's plan – we are saved to bear fruit; created in Christ Jesus for good works (Eph 2:10). We bear fruit when Christ lives His life in and through us (Jn 15:5; Gal 2:20). The apostle Paul said, "For me, to live is Christ, and to die is gain"

(Phil 1:21). The Lord wants us to live a godly and spiritually productive happy life. The world's philosophy says live for self... but god's word says die to self! Many people came to Jesus and asked to be His disciples, but most of them turned away because they were not willing to give themselves to Christ; i.e., make themselves a "slave of Christ"(Lk 14:26, 33; 16:13; Rom 12:1; 1 Cor 6:19-20; 1 Pet 1:18-19). Jesus said, "He who loves his father or mother or himself more than Me, he is not worthy of Me" (Mt 10:37-39). Thus Paul said, "I have been crucified with Christ; it is no longer I who live, but Christ lives in me" (Gal 2:20).

To many of us planting a seed looks no different than burying it. Both involve digging; both put the seed into the ground and cover it with soil, and both involve dying, yet only one has a destiny. You bury the dead to discard the body, but you plant a seed for it to come back greater than when it entered the ground. Even though you may be going through challenging times right now, remember that you've been planted, not buried. It may appear dark, cold, wet and uncomfortable, and you may have been in the ground for a long time, but cancel the florist and tell the preacher you're cancelling your funeral, because you're not dead, you're ready to be launched into your destiny. The ground that you're now in, though cold and wet is not meant to kill you but to make you strong. God is making your seed indestructible and able to grow in any type of environment, no matter how tough. Peter the beloved apostle reminds us in 1 Peter 1:23:

> For you have been born again, *not of perishable seed*, but of *imperishable* [seed], through the living and enduring Word of God.

As a part of the growth process you may have to be positioned in the 'dirt' but remember you are an imperishable seed, with a great future ahead. Your enemies thought they buried you, but they were wrong; they planted you. Joseph's brothers thought they buried him in the pit to die, but instead they planted him and he sprouted up in the palace. They thought they buried Jesus in the tomb, but He was the seed planted that sprung up into a harvest of souls unto everlasting life. That which the enemy planned for your death will be the very thing that will launch you into your destiny. To be planted is destiny concealed, and to have increase is destiny revealed. Your purpose might be concealed, but if you stay in the ground until it's time to bloom—if you stay in God's hand, it won't be long before your amazing purpose will be revealed.

## The seed needs to be watered

*O*nce the seed is planted the farmer waters it regularly. The Bible gives us an idyllic picture of God coming down to commune with Adam, the man-seed he planted in the Garden of Eden. After God placed him in the Garden He watered him (metaphorically speaking) with His presence. In the same way your seed which is your purpose needs to be watered, refreshed, rehearsed, visualized and realized while in fellowship with God in the secret place. Between the destiny concealed and the destiny revealed is the watering process—the last step before the increase and budding of the seed. As such it is a very important process. Watering is the transition point between what is concealed and what is about to be revealed. This describes the miraculous transformation from death unto life, so to speak.

Paul said, "I planted the seed, Apollos watered it, but God has been making it grow." All the seeds and plants in God's garden need continual, consistent watering. In Luke 8:6 Jesus said of the stony ground upon which the seed fell, "It lacked moisture." He went on to say that the seed "had no root" (Matt. 13:6). If the seed is to grow, the ground must be kept moist. It is because of the lack of constant watering that many of God's plants are withered and dying instead of growing and thriving. A garden is a place for growth. Paul wrote to the Thessalonians, "Your faith is growing exceedingly." (2 Thess. 1:3) God commanded all of us to "grow in grace." Therefore, God says to every one of His little gardens, "Be filled with the Spirit"–keep the ground moist. The water is the Spirit "whom God hath given to them that obey Him" (Acts 5:32). The fullness of the Spirit is the condition necessary for Him to do His perfect work. It is through the watering of the Spirit and the Word that your destiny is shaped.

*L*ebanon's cedars are symbolic of the Christian,

in that *they owe their planting entirely to the Lord*. Lebanon's cedars do not depend upon man for water; they stand on the lofty rock, untouched by human irrigation systems; and yet our heavenly Father supplies them. So it is with the Christian who has learned to live according to God's purpose for his life. He is not influenced by man's actions and opinions, even in temporal things, for his continued sustenance he looks to the Lord his God, and to Him alone. The dew of heaven is his portion, and the God of heaven is his fountain. Again, note that the cedars of Lebanon *are not protected by any mortal power*. They owe nothing to man for their protection from stormy winds and tempest. They are God's trees, kept and preserved by Him, and by Him alone. It is precisely the same with the Christian. He is not a hothouse plant, sheltered from temptation; he stands out in the elements; he has no shelter, no protection, except this that the broad wings of the eternal God always cover the cedars that He Himself has planted. Like cedars, believers are *full of sap*, having enough vitality to stay green, even amidst the bitter winter snows.

I am grateful to God that He is the perfect gardener (See John 15:1). It was God who watered us even though we did not show much promise or potential for growth. It was God who watered us and cultivated us even though we rebelled against His purpose for our lives. It was God who watered us when family, friends and coworkers turned their backs on us. He did those things simply because He created you and He knows your value and the power of the purpose that is being nurtured inside you.

---

**The seed has to work in harmony with its Environment**

---

Location is important for a seed. It does not decide where its wants to be planted, because that is the job of the sower. As God's seed you cannot determine the environment where you will be planted but you can be certain that wherever He plants you, He will work out your purpose and bring forth your incredible destiny. Many of us use our situation or the circumstances of our birth as an excuse for our failure to succeed. If that's the case, we need to take a lesson from the seed that learns to work in harmony with the sun, the soil, and the rain that refreshes it. The seed is well aware that if its sticks with the program, it will be released, to grow, bloom and flourish. The seed is aware that it has nothing to do with the process, because it did not create its circumstances. It therefore does not (so to speak) complain and whine about its location, but rather it has faith in the process and comes into agreement with it. Our environment is the garden in which we must discover greatness. God is able and eager to build our purpose through the very environment that seems to be working against us.

The story of Joseph in Genesis 37–50 is a thrilling example of the way God uses adversity to abundantly bless us. I could write an entire book just on the life of Joseph, but because of time limitations, we will just focus on a few key events in his life that are pertinent to our discussion. To begin, Joseph had a lot of things going for him when he was young. He was handsome. He was the first son born to Jacob through Rachel, and because Rachel was his father's favorite wife he was his father's favorite son. He had incredible God-inspired dreams that let him know God had great plans for him. But then one day his entire life changed. Can you imagine how it must have felt to know your brothers hated you enough to sell or kill you in order to get rid of you? He was forced to leave the comfortable life he had known, full of love from his parents, and go out into the unknown. How frightening that must have been for a boy of seventeen, yet God had His hand on Joseph. God had a divine purpose for this young man. Joseph had no idea why God had chosen that particular direction until the very end, but he never seemed to waver, because he believed God was always in control. Joseph kept his eyes on God, and He used Joseph greatly. Though he was planted in harsh and potentially-destructive surroundings, he did not allow his circumstances to redefine God's original intention but chose to follow His leading. You were built and positioned to flourish wherever God has planted you. Take a look around you to discover the opportunities that God is using to work for your good.

## Breakthrough Seed

The final point I would like to make with the

seed metaphor is this: when the seed is planted it must face the first greatest barrier, the very ground where it is sown. That ground will attempt to reject it and envelope it in darkness, which promotes rot and degeneration; however, that are the very elements also necessary for growth, for with opposition comes from change and with change comes growth and adaptation. Since seeds need light and the roots need water, the seed begins the perpetual hunt for water (downward) and light (upward). Adversity is good, resistance is necessary, and opposition is cardinal! When we see these things occur, we should lift our head up high, find our way through and soldier on, without making the soil our home, for our light will break forth like the bright morning sun and our legacy shall be birthed like the springs of the mighty Zambezi River!

# Chapter 4

## IDENTIFYING YOUR PURPOSE

So far we've discussed the meaning of purpose and have established that we were created and planted for a purpose. Now we will turn our attention to the way we are to identify our God-given purpose. The two greatest days of our lives are the days we were born and the day we discover our purpose. But if we don't know our purpose, we don't know why we're here, which can make it hard to keep going. As a pastor and university professor I'm frequently asked, "How do I discover God's purpose for my life?" Many of us walk through life, feeling numb and desperate for a deeper connection, but often we're unsure how to get it. The truth is that we can't think our way into our life's passion and purpose; we have to 'do' our way in. This means taking steps toward what we want and removing things that don't move us toward our destiny.

If you've been around long, you've noticed the ongoing focus on discovering our God-given purpose in books, blogs, sermons; TV and radio programs and other media venues can make it seem impossible to discover our purpose. It can appear that God is playing hide and seek with our purpose just to tease us. But nothing could be further from the truth. In fact, Christ came into the world because God wants us to know Him and His deep love and longing to bless us. Seeing God's will realized in your life means, first of all, discovering the unique purpose for which He designed you. In nature, water always seeks the path of least resistance and our human nature does the same thing if we allow it to. On the other hand we can end up meandering through life, allowing obstacles we encounter to determine the direction we take. But it doesn't have to be that way. God wants us to experience the satisfaction of a life well lived. We can do this if we're willing to do more than just go with the flow—remember that even a dead fish can float downstream. Below are a number of practical steps to help you discover your purpose.

**Ask your Creator**

This might sound rather obvious but often we really do not take the time to actually seek God, asking for His purpose for our lives. The Bible says,

> "Seek first the kingdom of God and His righteousness and all other things will be given to you" (Matt. 6:33).

If you're already aware that you can ask, you might not know how to listen for God's response to your question.

The truth is that God wants you to know exactly why He created you, but you can only find answers in relationship with Him. The Bible gives us seven basic keys or filters through which every possible leading should be judged. We are to carefully examine the thoughts and intentions of our hearts and the words of godly people who may influence us: The seven keys:

1. Read the Bible

God usually communicates with us through His Word—the Bible. Take time to prayerfully read and study His Word and carefully listen to His voice:

> All Scripture is given by inspiration of God, and is profitable for doctrine, for reproof, for correction, for instruction in righteousness, that the man of God may be complete, thoroughly equipped for every good work (II Timothy 3:16-17).

---

Many of the thoughts that pop into our minds are from the Holy Spirit.

---

Saint Augustine asserts:

> Such is the depth of the Christian Scriptures that even if I were attempting to study them and nothing sled from early boyhood to decrepit old age, with the utmost leisure, the most unwearied zeal, and

talent greater that I have, I would still daily be making progress in discovering their treasure[18]

2. Listen to the Holy Spirit

The Holy Spirit is a person and as a person He speaks and communicates with us. As we go about our days, seeking to follow Jesus and love others, we must recognize that many of the thoughts that "pop into" our minds regarding the needs and concerns of others, are probably not our own thoughts, but are rather due to the quiet guidance of the Holy Spirit:

"For this is the covenant that I will make with the house of Israel after those days, says the Lord: I will put my laws into their minds, and I will write them on their hearts and I will be their God, and they shall be my people. And they shall not teach everyone his fellow citizen, and everyone his brother, saying, 'know the Lord,' for all will know Me, from the least to the greatest of them." (Hebrews 8:10-11). To be filled with the Spirit, according to Bill Bright, is to be filled with Christ. The Holy

[18] Arthur Flake, *Life At Eighty As I See It* (Nashville: Broadman Press, 1944), 97.

Spirit came to glorify Christ. Therefore, if I am filled with the Spirit, I am abiding in Christ…And if I am controlled and empowered by Christ, He will be walking around in my body, living His resurrection life I and through me.[19]

  3. Be open to God's prophetic word of knowledge, word of wisdom, or personal prophecy

Sometimes God will use trusted leaders and pastors to speak a prophetic word to you. Listen and discern to determine whether it confirms what God has already been stirring in your spirit.

"Do not quench the Spirit; do not despise prophetic utterances. But examine everything carefully; hold fast to that which is good" (I Thessalonians 5:19-21).

  4. Listen to godly counsel

Ask trusted friends what they believe your purpose is. As a young man I preached my first message at my local church at the age of seventeen. I was surprised when my pastor told me that God

---

[19] Bill Bright, *How To Be Filled With the Spirit and His Gifts* (Grand Rapids, MI: Zondervan Publishing Co., 1970), 72.

was going to use me to preach His Word all over the world. His words inspired me because I trusted him. That was the purpose moment that unfolded into my life's purpose.

> Where no counsel is, the people fall: but in the multitude of counselors there is safety. (Prov. 11:14)

### 5.  Connect the confirmation dots

Listen to confirmations from various sources such as God's Word, prophecies, words of knowledge, general encouragements, and so on. These may be important confirmation as to your purpose and calling.

By the mouth of two or three witnesses every fact may be confirmed (Matt. 18:16).

### 6.  Embrace the peace of God

I was shocked when, sitting in my office in 1995, I heard the Holy Spirit say I was to move to West Africa to work as a missionary. Even though it was a daunting and overwhelming undertaking I felt a peace that was past my understanding.

Let the peace of Christ rule in your hearts, to which indeed you were called in one body; and be thankful (Col. 3:15). An old Poem say:

> In the center of the whirlpool, while the waters rush around,
>
> There's a space of perfect stillness, though with turmoil it is bound;
>
> All is calm, and all is quiet, scarcely e'en a sense of sound,
>
> So with us—despite the conflict—when in Christ His peace is found.[20]

7. Observe the circumstances and timing: Divine timing is defined this way: When God is in control everything happens at its exact right time. I like to think of it as the time it takes from the moment I receive an epiphany or inspired thought regarding the plan to when this plan is manifested in reality. In this modern age of multi-tasking, high-speed wireless Internet and increasingly intricate information superhighways, people have gotten used to getting whatever they want whenever they want it. But things are different in God's economy. He is in no hurry, so we must learn to be patient and wait on

---

[20] Charles E Cowman, Spring in the Valley (Los Angeles: Cowman Publications, inc., 1939), 138.

Him for the right timing.

> After these things he (Paul) left Athens and went to Corinth. And he found a certain Jew named Aquila, a native of Pontus, having recently come from Italy with his wife Priscilla, because Claudius had commanded all the Jews to leave Rome. He came to them, and because he was of the same trade, he stayed with them and they were working; for by trade they were tentmakers (Acts 18:1-3).  This relationship between Paul, Aquila and Priscilla, which happened as a result of circumstances--became one of the most important strategic partnerships in the entire book of Acts).

**Practical Tips for identifying your Purpose**
**Meet a Need**

Whether you know your purpose or not there is

still much you can do. Do you see people around you with needs you can meet? Does your church need ushers or greeters? Does your family need spiritual guidance or practical help? Are there opportunities to volunteer in your local community? Find a need and meet it. Of course it would be good if it's an activity you don't despise, and it's even better if it's something you can enjoy. The fact is that we often tap into our passion when we begin meeting the needs of those around us. Frederick Buechner was insightful when he said,

> "The place God calls you to is the place where your deep gladness and the world's deep hunger meet." [21]

So use your talents to meet the needs of those around you, and not only will you find deep satisfaction, but you may even discover your destiny!


## Do what you're wired to do

I remember asking a pastor how he knew God

had called him to pastor a church. He said he

---

[21] Frederick Buechner, *Wishful Thinking: A Theological ABC* (Harper & Row, 1973), 10.

never heard a heavenly voice tell him to go pastor a church, but rather he just did what he was wired to do. He was wired to pastor a church. God wired him a certain way and he simply moved in that anointing. He didn't seek his purpose. Rather, he was already fulfilling it simply by doing what God wired him to do. You can do the same thing.

Why not simply live according to the way that God wired you instead of spending hours and days trying to discover the plan. The way you're wired may be found in the things you like or the things you feel comfortable doing. God has already wired you for a particular task—just do it! One day you'll realize that you're already operating in your gift and that you have therefore discovered your God-given purpose.

I believe this is the best way to discover our special, one-of-a-kind answers. That is to realize that God has already prepared you for exactly what He wants you to do. He has already wired you a certain way so all you have to do is operate according to the way you are made. Your purpose has already been established and is already inside of you just waiting for you to unlock it.

The discovery you seek is really just an identification of what you already are. We seem to like titles. If we would just operate according to the way God wired us we wouldn't have to worry about identifying our purpose because we would find that we operate in it without even thinking. The only thing we may need is instruction for the purpose of edification. For example, a person gifted as an evangelist might want to talk to other more experienced evangelists to learn more.

To review, just live according to the way God made you and you will by default fulfill your God-given purpose. If you live in obedience to God, your path will be established in Christ and you won't have to worry about identifying your purpose because you will already be living it. It's important to simply do what we already know to do before we spend time trying to discover what God wants us to do. Our first priority is to be a disciple of Christ, then to preach the gospel according to the way God designed us, to bear fruit, to love each other, to practice the ministry of reconciliation and to walk by the Spirit of God. There are many 'jobs' for you to do in God's Kingdom that are not specifically stated in the Bible. The important thing is to simply be in fellowship with God and to be what He made you, doing what He has already wired you to do.

The apostle Peter gives us this admonition in 1 Peter 4:10:

> As each one has received a gift, minister it to one another, as good stewards of the manifold grace of God.

God has equipped every one of us to perform a special mission for which we alone were created. And while it's a great accomplishment to discover our gifts, it's not enough. After you know what you're naturally gifted to do and how you're hard wired you have to place yourself in a position to use that talent.[22]

So, when you seek to discover God's will for your life, pay attention to how He has gifted you. His plan for you will always be directly related to the gifts He has bestowed upon you. The great news is that you will automatically be good at whatever it is that He called you to do!

---

[22] Bob McDonald, *Don't Waste Your Talent* (NY: The Highlands Company, 2005), ii

**Listen to the Holy Spirit.**

I used to pray and pray without giving the Holy Spirit a chance to respond. I was used to doing all the talking when I prayed. But then, several years ago, I read Bill Hybel's book, *Too Busy Not to Pray*. That book completely changed the way I approached God through prayer. Since reading that book, I have added a significant and formerly-missing component to my prayer life: listening. Now I take time to listen to what God wants to say to me.

I experienced a major turning point in my own prayer life when I simply learned to shut up while I was praying. That may sound odd to you; it certainly did as Bill Hybel explained:

> *We serve a God who has spoken in history, who will indeed speak tomorrow and who wants to speak to us right now, right here where we are.*[23]

Those who are truly interested in hearing from

---

[23] Bill Hybel, *Too Busy Not to Pray* (Downer Grove, IL: IVP, 2008), 137.

God understand that there's a price to be paid—
*disciplined stillness.* God actually tries to communicate with us more often than we know.

**Listen to your heart.**

In addition to listening to the Spirit, it's also important to listen to your heart. To understand my
point here, consider the following passage:

> Delight yourself also in the LORD, and
> He shall give you the desires of your heart.
> Commit your way to the LORD, trust also
> in Him, and He shall bring it to pass (Ps.
> 37:4-5 NKJV).

As we draw near to God in prayer and meditation
He will actually begin to shape and influence our
desires toward the things He has called us to do.
In God we are to trust, waiting, resting, taking
great delight in, committing ourselves to knowing Him, and choosing to have patience. If we
delight in Him we will experience His peace, sta-
bility, provision, guidance and protection, as
well as deliverance, firm footing, a secure future,
a refuge, a worry-free life and abundant bless-
ings. And above all He will give us the desires
of our hearts, which He Himself placed inside us.

# Chapter 5
# PURPOSE AND RELATIONSHIPS

Relationships are at the core of who we are as humans. From Shakespearian dramas to the current top ten music charts, nearly every artistic expression focuses on relationship: songs of love lost and found, tales of our deepest longings and greatest tragedies. Whether it is an individual broken heart, or whole families and societies devastated by relationships gone bad, relationships reflect our deepest human struggles. They are the source of our most profound joy and our deepest pain. Relationships are the things we are willing to kill and die for—what we long for most—what keep us up at night. It is in relationship that we find out who we are as humans, and what matters most in life.

Relationship is at the heart of the Christian faith, reflecting the fact that we as humans have been made for relationship. Jesus identifies the central message of the law and prophets relationally Matthew 22: 36-40 tells us:

> "Teacher, which is the greatest commandment in the law?" Jesus said to him, "You shall love the Lord your God with all your heart, with all your soul, and with all your mind.' This is the first and great commandment. And the second is like it: 'You shall love your neighbor as yourself.' On these two commandments hang all the Law and the Prophets."

From love to hate, relationship also encompasses the depths of sin and the heights of moral virtue: including compassion, sacrifice, forgiveness, trust, betrayal, murder, adultery, revenge. Each is deeply rooted in relationship. It is at the heart of both ethics and worship. All throughout Christianity's history, relationship has been the heartbeat of a vibrant faith. We see it in the aching prose of Augustine's "Confessions", the wounded and intimate visions of Julian of Norwich's "Revelations of Divine Love", and the stirring chords of John Newton's "Amazing Grace." It fills both the pages of hymnals and the shelves of Christian bookstores.

### The most valuable relationship of all

In order to comprehend the true meaning and purpose of our relationships, we must begin with our most primary relationship of all. One in particular provides the greater context for all our other relationships at all levels. It is in this one relationship that we find our beginning and our final resting place. It is the one relationship that establishes our purpose for being in the world, the value of our growth and development and the direction and aim of all of our contributions as long as we live. It is the relationship that is most essential to our well-being and our understanding of ourselves, and the world. Yet it is the relationship to which we may give the least attention. Some of us may not have considered it at all. In fact, we may never have given it much serious thought. I'm referring to our relationship with God.[24] Our purpose is revealed in relationship with God. When we seek the God of our

---

[24] Marshall Van Summers, Relationship and Higher Purpose (New Knowledge Library, 2013), 11

purpose we will find our purpose in the process.

Biblical destiny originates with God and is communicated to human beings.
For instance: After spending forty years on the backside of a desert, Moses had His "burning bush" experience with God. It was here that God made it very clear what He wanted Moses to do. At that point Moses was forced to decide whether to do God's will and embrace his destiny or to reject it. Also, it's important to know that when the plan comes from God…it works! It can't fail if we walk in it…Why? Because it's from God – Isa. 55:11 NLT tells us, "It is the same with MY word. I send it out…and it will always accomplish what I want it to…" In other words, His plans never fail to accomplish His will.

In his book, *Relationship and Higher Purpose*, Marshall van Summers explains that in everyday lives, our relationship with God is usually the last thing on the list, taking a distant backseat to everything else. When real meaning, purpose and value are not clearly defined, people assign value to their relationships based upon their own immediate needs, preferences and understanding. This is how we establish false substitutes for true meaning, purpose and value. That's why it's so difficult for most people to discern the value of their own relationships.[25]

It's vital that we base our understanding of the relationship between ourselves and God upon the foundational truth that we were born with a specific purpose planned by God before the world began. Once we are clear about that we can soak in the secret place of God, seeking His perspective on that particular plan for our lives, and He will reveal everything we need to equip us for service. Of course this can only occur once we receive His great gift of salvation, asking Him to forgive our sins and restore the relationship between us.

It's vital that we know our purpose, because it is the premise upon which we must build as we seek to go deeper in relationship to God.[26]

The emphasis here, as van Summers so aptly explains it, is for us to reach that vantage point where we can clearly see and understand the relationship between us and God while we

---

[25] Ibid.
[26] Ibid.

*pursue* our God-given purpose once He reveals it. Like climbing a great mountain we must reach the place where the relationship of that mountain to everything around it becomes crystal clear. From that vantage point, we will see clearly why we were never able to understand before.
*Me, Myself and I*

As strange as it may sound it's also vital that we

have a healthy relationship with ourselves in order to discover our purpose. To borrow van Summers' example, the 'self' is made up of the mind and the body. The mind is the thinking mechanism that controls the body and the control center from which our mind operates. This is important because it is in the arena of mind and body where healing and empowerment takes place. Proverbs 23:7a tells us, "For as he thinks in his heart, so is he." "A man is what he thinks about all day long," says Ralph Waldo Emerson. Our life is what our thoughts make it," adds, Marcus Aurelius. Our defeat or victory begins with what we think, and if we guard our thoughts we shall not have much trouble anywhere else along the line, says Vance Havner.[27] An important aspect of finding our purpose is therefore our thoughts, particularly the way we subconsciously speak about ourselves.

What enables us to find our real purpose, meaning and direction is our ability to represent the Greater Power—God who sent us into the world. What gives our body purpose, meaning and direction is its service to our mind. What gives our mind purpose, meaning and direction is its service to our existence. What gives our existence purpose, meaning and direction is its service to God. And what gives God purpose, meaning and direction is when we live and move and have our being to express His heart. In other words the way we relate to ourselves must be with a clear view of our identity in Christ, so that we live to do His will, expressing His majesty, wisdom and splendor—His glory, in all we do and say. It is for this reason Paul admonishes:

> I beseech you therefore, brethren, by the mercies of God, that you present your bodies a living sacrifice, holy, acceptable to God, which is your reasonable service.

---

[27] Vance Harvner, *Pleasant Paths* (Grand Rapids, MI: Baker Book House, 1945), 72.

> And do not be conformed to this world,
> but be transformed by the renewing of
> your mind, that you may prove what is
> that good and acceptable and perfect will
> of God. (Romans 12:1-2)

Once we see that we are desperately loved, forgiven and restored to fellowship with God we can love ourselves (body, mind and spirit) enough to walk in those truths, in service to others and to God.

*The Ubuntu principle*

Often our purpose/destiny is bound together with that of someone else. This could be a spouse or a covenant relationship with a friend or mentor. This is the idea behind the Ubuntu principle. Ubuntu is a Zulu African word that captures the spirit and philosophical foundation for African living. It is a unifying vision or worldview enshrined in the Zulu maxim *umuntu ngumuntu ngabantu*, i.e., "a person is a person through other persons." The essence of this African aphorism is the fundamental connectivity between people. It asserts that our ability to co-exist goes

to the very core of our humanity. A longer definition by Archbishop Desmond Tutu says this:

> "A person with Ubuntu is open and avail-
> able to others, affirming of others, does
> not feel threatened that others are able and
> good, for he or she has a proper self-assur-
> ance that comes from knowing that he or
> she belongs in a greater whole and is di-
> minished when others are humiliated or
> diminished, when others are tortured or
> oppressed."

Each of us was designed with a specific purpose
which is our calling in life. As such, we must
choose those we associate with, because over
time we become like them in thought, word and
deed. With that in mind, let me say that unless
specifically directed by God, we are not to be
closely associated with those who could lead us
into error. Those closest to us should be of like
precious faith, because we want those who influence us to be pleasing to God, so that iron sharp-
ens iron. For this reason, we must examine our
hearts to determine our motives for questionable

relationships, and seek God's wisdom and direction to pull away from those that don't ultimately lead us into a deeper walk with God.

**Covenant Relationships**
This is especially true when we are choosing a life-partner. When it pertains to pursuing God's purpose we do not need fair-weather friends but rather we need a covenant relationship that will help us grow into the people we are destined to be. Below is a list of covenant relationships that are purpose-oriented:

(1) **The covenant of affirmation**... There is nothing you have done or will do that will make me stop loving you. This godlike love takes the initiative to affirm and not give up. Like Jesus, "He appointed twelve, to be with Him." Mark 3:14

(2) **The covenant of availability** . . . I am committed to going beyond myself, anything I have--time, energy, insight, possessions--is at your disposal if you need it to the limit of my resources.

Everything Jesus had was available to His disciples. He committed himself and His resources to a few, regardless of inconvenience or cost.

(3) **The covenant of prayer** . . . I promise to pray regularly for you, believing that our caring Father wants His children to pray for one another. In Peter's temptation, Jesus said, "I have prayed for you that your faith fail not."

(4) **The covenant of openness** . . . I promise to be a more open person . . . disclosing my feelings, hopes, and longings. The degree to which I do so implies that I cannot make it without you . . . that I trust you with my problems and dreams. Jesus openly expressed His love for His disciples. In the Garden, He honestly admitted His needs and asked for prayer.

(5) **The covenant of honesty** . . . I will try to "mirror" back to you what I am hearing you say and feel. I will

risk "speaking the truth in love that we grow up in every way unto Christ who is the head." (Eph. 4:15)

(6) **The covenant of sensitivity** . . . I promise to be sensitive to you and your needs to the best of my ability. I will try to hear you--see you--anticipate where you are--and draw you out of the pit of discouragement or withdrawal. It costs to be sensitive. Jesus confronted Peter in John 21:15-17 and reconciliation took place. Sometimes through the eyes another person, we see ourselves more clearly.

(7) **The covenant of confidentiality** . . . I promise to keep confidential the things we share in order to provide an atmosphere of openness. Why is confidentiality so important? There can be no love without trust. When we trust others, we can open up to love, to give and receive. Confidentiality opens the door to deeper relation-

ships. James 5:16 tells us to: "Confess your faults to one another, and pray for one another, that you may be healed."

(8) **The covenant of accountability** . . . I promise, that if I discover areas of my life that are under bondage, hung-up, or being misused, I will seek Christ's liberating power through His Holy Spirit . . . I will be accountable to you to become what God has designed me to be. Accountability is the foundation of any love covenant for it recognizes when there is a problem and gives permission to share with others. Out of accountability flows the love, acceptance and forgiveness we need. The relationship helps us to work out a plan of action. It is truly a beautiful thing to be able to say, "What happens to me matters to you."

## Lessons from Naomi, Ruth and Boaz

*N*aomi was married to Elemelech (meaning God is King) and they had two sons *Mahlon* and *Chilion.* They migrated to the land of Moab because of famine in Judah, where eventually the sons married Ruth and Orpah who were Moabites (Non- Hebrews). Within ten years Elemelech and his sons died, leaving Naomi, (the mother in-law), Ruth and Orpah (her daughter in-laws) to fend for themselves. On hearing that the famine had subsided in Judah Naomi decided to head back home. (She had left Judah with a husband and two sons and was returning home with her daughters-in-law.) While they were getting ready to leave to return to Judah (a foreign and hostile place for any Moabite), Naomi realized the sacrifice the girls were making out of loyalty to her. It was highly unlikely that a Hebrew man would marry a Moabite woman. After beseeching them to go back to Moah, Orpah decided to return home to Moab after many tears, but *Ruth clung to Naomi, refusing to let her go:*

> Entreat me not to leave you,
> Or turn back from following after you;

For wherever you go, I will go;
And wherever you lodge, I will lodge;
Your people shall be my people,
And your God, my God
Where you die, I will die;
And there will I be buried
The Lord do so to me, and more also,
If anything but death parts you and me
(Ruth 1:16-17)

Ruth realized that her future, her purpose and her destiny were bound up with Naomi's. Even though her future looked bleak she realized that the covenant relationship she shared with Naomi went far beyond the circumstances of their current predicament. Ruth's loyalty to Naomi was later rewarded when she later met and married a wealth godly businessman by the name of Boaz.

# Chapter 6

## *PURPOSE IN THE MIDST OF CRISIS*

*O*ne the surprising obstacles to us find-ing and living on purpose is that we usually ex-pect it to be problem free. Often we see opposi-tion as a sign that this is not something we should be doing, but nothing could be further from the truth. People who live out their purpose have to learn to ride on the wings of adversity.

---

Learning to deal with discouragement is part of the process of finding and living out our purpose.

---

We fail to realize that the only way to build our Purpose muscle is to stretch and exercise our faith. Helen Keller said, "Life is either a daring adventure, or it is nothing at all." Those words would ring true no matter who said them, but coming from someone who lived with profound disabilities, they deserve our special consideration. Born blind, deaf and unable to speak, she somehow found a way out of the darkness and into the world around her. Her story is one of the great miracles of the twentieth century. Millions of people have drawn inspiration from her example. When we inject her statement into our discussion about purpose it looks something like this: *The life of purpose is inherently a life of risk.* Go back to the Bible and take a look at the men and women who lived out their purpose. Almost without exception, they were risk-takers who weren't afraid to lay it all on the line for God. Consider these examples:

- Noah built an ark though he had never seen it rain.
- Abraham left Ur of the Chaldees without knowing his destination.
- Moses led the people of God out of Egypt.

- Joshua marched around the walls of Jericho.
- David defeated Goliath.
- Elijah faced down the prophets of Baal.
- Esther risked everything to save her people.
- Daniel refused to defile himself with the king's food.
- Nehemiah led the Jews to rebuild the walls of Jerusalem.

When you read the Bible, again and again you discover that the men and women who accomplished great things for God and lived out their purpose were not content to accept the status quo. Instead they listened to their hearts and dared to be different. When we choose to live out our purpose we will face opposition, roadblocks, setbacks and discouragement. Learning to deal with discouragement is part of the process of finding and living out our purpose.

*Purpose in the midst of adversity: Lessons on purpose from Jeremiah the weeping Prophet*

Jeremiah was living through tough times. The northern kingdom had already fallen and Daniel, the three Hebrew boys and all of Israel were taken into captivity. These were hard times! On the surface it appeared that God's purpose for Israel and Judah was in tatters. However it is often through the ashes of life that God builds our purpose and shapes our character. At the darkest moment of the lives of God's chosen people, when all hope had been dashed, God told the Prophet Jeremiah to go down to the potter's house:

The word of the Lord came to Jeremiah saying, arise and go down to the Potters House, there I will cause you to hear my words" (Jeremiah 18: 1-2).

I am intrigued thinking about the various ways and means God uses to share His heart with us. God goes to great lengths to teach and to communicate to us using many kinds of object lessons. Sometimes when we stray off our purpose trail the Lord will allow us to face situations and circumstances to get us back on track. When we find ourselves in situations where we feel like we've gone off on a tangent, we must pay attention because God may be trying to teach us something, just like He did with Jeremiah.

God commanded Jeremiah to:

> Arise and go down to the Potters House and THERE I will cause you to HEAR (V. 2) (Emphasis mine).

The first thing to notice is that God desires to use His Word to get us back on course toward our purpose. Secondly, God will use our environment to work for us. God commanded him to go to a specific location where Jeremiah could hear Him above the clamor of Israel's rebellion. Notice also that He did not say, "Go there because I am going to show you something", but rather, "I am going to cause you to hear." This is important because quite often God causes us to hear something far different from what we see. Romans 10:17 says this: "Faith comes by hearing." This is a very important lesson to learn if we are diverted from our God-given purpose because of challenges in our lives. Stop and listen to that inner voice of God that you once heard clearly. Our trying situations will take us to the place where we can hear the voice of the Holy Spirit. It was only when Jacob was in a complete bind that he was willing to hear the Lord speak. Before him was his brother fuming with revenge and behind him Laban was seeking to kill him (See Genesis 32). God had a destiny for Jacob to fulfill but during that time he was living outside of God's purpose so God used that trying situation to show him who he really was--a prince. If we are seemingly far outside of God's purpose for our lives we need to look around because God is actually very close by trying to get our attention.

Jeremiah went down early in the morning and the first thing he would have seen is the potter going out with a wheelbarrow to dig something from the dirt. From that word picture it's clearly evident which of them was the Creator and the which was the created. What are the basic ingredients of clay? Dust mixed with water. We as human beings are of the dust (Ps.103:14), but when mixed with the water of the Spirit of God we come to life through faith in Christ. When we find ourselves living outside our purpose we must recognize that it was God who took us from the dirt, put His spirit into us and gave us our purpose. Our purpose is therefore not of our choosing but is of God who is our master Creator. The first thing God wanted to establish for Jeremiah was who was the boss, who was in charge--who was the potter and who was the clay. Jeremiah grew weary when the people refused to receive his message. On one occasion the persecution grew too much for Jeremiah and he decided he would not preach anymore because things weren't not going as he expected. (See Jer. 20:9.) God was teaching him and Israel the importance of submission. Jeremiah saw clearly that the clay was subject to the potter, and as much as we might not want to hear it, this truth applies to us as well.

Accompanying this rebuke however was the affirmation that they (Israel) were loved and had been chosen. In spite of Israel's failure they were still the chosen people of God. This is a word for us also. In spite of our weaknesses and failures God has still chosen us to fulfill His purposes on earth.

Jeremiah would have noticed that in order to make clay the potter had to find clay that was just the right blend of earth and water. If it contained too much water the clay would be too wet and fail to harden. If it's too soft it will break with the first use, good for nothing. If it is too dry it will crumble, completely useless. The formula had to have the exact amounts of soil and water to be made into beautiful vessels. God chose you because you are usable and pliable in His hand. In spite of your failures and shortcomings you are just the person for the job He has called you to.

*The Kneading Process*

Once the potter mixed the right amounts of both earth and water the clay, Jeremiah observed the kneading process. The reason for the kneading process is two-fold—first of all, to remove all the air bubbles. Any air pockets left in the clay will cause the piece to explode during firing in the kiln. Secondly, any grit or foreign particles remaining in the clay will create imperfections and cause the clay to weaken and to fall apart when it is being thrown on the potter's wheel. The potter can feel these in the clay as he works it with his hands.

In order to be used by God for His purpose, all the junk, all the imperfections, all the sin, all of self, must be removed from our lives. God cannot **use us** if there is still some **of us in us!**

Jeremiah continued to observe the Potter making SOMETHING at the wheel.

And THERE, he was making *SOME-THING* at the wheel.

At first Jeremiah had no idea what the potter was making. Like the lump of clay your purpose might be unformed and undeveloped so that's it's hard to determine, but remember you're still in the potter's hand. As long as we stay in His hand God will be able to create something wonderful and purposeful in our lives.

Jeremiah would have noticed that the potter was not improvising or simply making something on the fly without a plan. Absolutely not! The potter not only had a perfect plan for the clay but could already visualize the finished product in his mind, setting in motion a perfect process. Paul says:

> For we are His workmanship, created in Christ Jesus for good works, which God prepared beforehand so that we would walk in them (Eph. 2:10).

It is also written:

> For I am confident of this very thing, that
> He who began a good work in you will
> perfect it until the day of Christ Jesus
> (Phil.1:6).

Although we might not be able to see the finished product, God has already envisioned its purpose and promises a quality result. Just as it is written,

> Things which eye has not seen and ear has
> not heard,
> And which have not entered the heart of
> man,
> All that God has prepared for those who
> love Him. (1 Cor. 2:9)

Jeremiah knew God was making SOMETHING because the "wheel was still turning." As long as the wheel is still turning you're still in the game. When the wheel is turning it means there is a relationship between the potter and the clay. It means God is still on the job. There is a song we use to sing back in the day that says:

*Please be patient with me God is not
through with me yet
Please be patient with me God is not
through with me yet
When God gets through with me
When God gets through with me
I shall come forth
I shall come forth as pure gold.*

As long as the clay stays responsive in the potter's hand and responsive to the potter's touch its
intended purpose will be realized. God is the
Potter. I don't think there's any doubt about that.
If there is, check out Isaiah 64:8:

> "But now, O LORD, thou art our father;
> we are the clay, and thou art our potter."

It couldn't be plainer. It is the potter who molds
and shapes the clay. He knows exactly what He
wants the finished product to look like. The clay
is totally under his control. It must be 100%
yielded to him, not 50%, or even 99%. The clay
MUST YIELD to the potter's hand if it is to become something useful. We yield to God by sur-
rendering our will. In the same way that clay
cannot mold itself, only God has the power to
properly shape and guide us into our purpose.

The message of verses 6-10 is that God the Potter is sovereign over the clay. The clay needs to submit to the Potter in order to be formed into something useful according to His will.

*Messed up, but still on the wheel*

The vessel he made of clay was marred in his hand. (Jer. 18:4)

Jeremiah continued to watch and realized that the clay became marred in the potter's hand. Notice that it was marred while in the potter's hand. Being in the Potter's hand does not mean we are free from trials and tribulations. Sometimes our purpose gets out of focus because of 'life'. Too often when people 'mess up' we are apt to discard them. But God is not like that; when we fail and our purpose appears to be shipwrecked He doesn't throw us away on the rubbish heap of failed potential.

V. 4 …so, he made it again into another vessel.

He is a God of the second chance. Just when our

enemies thought we were through, when they declared that we were down for the count we see him working on "another vessel." When you feel deep down that you have missed your season or you are outside of the intended will of God, please know it is not too late. If you stay in His hand God can use the same MESS that brought you to your knees and turn it into a MESSAGE.

What tool would you expect Jeremiah to have seen in a potter's workshop, one that seems to be missing, yet was probably implied? There's no mention of a furnace or kiln, which is crucial to the finished product. No clay vessel is worth anything until it's gone through the furnace. Everyone who pursues God's purpose also must go through fire to be purified. Job says:

> But He knows the way I take;
> When He has tried me, I shall come forth
> as gold (Job 23:10).

Isaiah says:

> "Behold, I have refined you, but not as
> silver; I have tested you in the furnace of
> affliction" (Isa. 48:10).

Peter asserts:

> Beloved, do not be surprised at the fiery ordeal among you, which comes upon you for your testing, as though some strange thing were happening to you; but to the degree that you share the sufferings of Christ, keep on rejoicing, so that also at the revelation of His glory you may rejoice with exultation. (1 Peter 4:12-13)

When it comes to trials, we must yield to the Potter, allowing Him to have His way in order to become a vessel destined for His divine purpose.

Life's "fiery trials"—debt and divorce, decay and disorder, pain and death—afflict us all. But we have the consolation that there's an eternal purpose behind it all. Ellen White notes:

> "The fact that we are called upon to endure trial shows that the Lord Jesus sees in us something precious which He desires to develop.... He does not cast

*The hotter the furnace, the finer the vessel.*

Earthenware, though brightly-colored and glazed, chips easily if it is baked at lower temperatures. Such vessels have none of the inner strength needed to withstand pressure or vigorous service. Stoneware, much harder and stronger, bakes in a furnace nearly twice as hot as that for earthenware. But porcelain, baked between 2400 and 2700 degrees Fahrenheit, is the finest and most expensive type of pottery.

Yet a potter doesn't arbitrarily require an inordinate amount of endurance from any of his vessels. Indeed, different kinds of pots require different levels of heat; in the Master Potter's house no vessel receives more heat than it needs. Still, it does take a "fiery trial" to produce fine pottery, and the product of the greatest "pain" is

---

[28] Ellen White, *The Ministry of Healing* (Mountain View, CA: Pacific Press Publishing Association, 1942), 471.

97

porcelain, that produces a characteristic "ring" when hit. Like John Huss and Jerome, who sang while being burned at the stake, or Paul and Silas, who sang in a Philippian jail, Christians are human porcelain. Day by day through the Spirit, believers develop this Christ-like resonance, this total rejection of revenge, this ability to love under pressure as we live out our purpose in the world.

Upon His wheel, through His Spirit, the Master Potter can shape us. He sees us not as "marred clay," but as fine porcelain in the making. He promises to restore us to His original design and purpose. And because "[He] is faithful … he will do it" (1 Thess. 5:24, NIV).

**Chapter 7**

***FOLLOW YOUR PASSION***

*"Every great dream begins with a dreamer. Always remember, you have within you the strength, the patience, and the passion to reach for the stars to change the world."* - Harriet Tubman

**O**ur God is a passionate God. He passionately loves some things and passionately hates others. As we grow closer to Him, He'll share His passion with us. You could say that God's passion becomes His purpose. This may be passion about helping people, building something, solving a problem or bringing joy to others. What makes godly passion so infectious is that we're communicating something that makes God smile—something He is passionate about. When we find our passion we will find our purpose.



To be passionate about something means to be acutely interested in it, willing to put substantial energy into promoting it, willing to sacrifice for it, and hardly able to keep from talking about it. God places His passion within us when He gives us the Holy Spirit. But it lies dormant unless we present our bodies to Him as a living sacrifice. In other words, God brings His passion to life in those who are willing to sacrifice. Those who present themselves a living sacrifice are always passionate about spiritual things whereas those who are self-centered tend to be indifferent or apathetic about God. Many people are somewhere in between; they sacrifice very little and therefore have little passion. But they are not really on fire about anything. When Paul told Timothy to "stir up the gift" that was within him (2

Tim. 1:6), he was telling him to stop being timid and to do the will of God, even if it cost him something. God's fire falls on a properly-prepared sacrifice.

You know when you're passionate about something, because usually you can't stop talking about it or thinking about it. Jesus said, "A man's heart determines his speech" (Matt. 12:34 ). Passion inspires fire in your belly and drives you out of bed each morning. People are passionate or zealous about many things. We are passionate about sports teams, careers, travel, children, hobbies and our special interests. People usually have enough time, energy and money for the things about which they're passionate.

The big question is: 'Are we passionate about that which is most important?' Are we passionate about God? The harsh truth is that anything that trumps our passion for God *is an idol*. Although in this piece we're discussing regarding passion in relation to purpose, we ensure that our passions are godly when we focus our ultimate affection on God. The Bible has much to say about our 'zeal' for God. In Numbers 25:11 God speaks of "Phinehas, the son of Eleazar, the son of Aaron the priest, hath turned my wrath away from the children of Israel, while he was zealous for my sake among them, that I consumed not the children of Israel in my jealousy." Here God describes Himself as passionate and zealous. Several times in the Old Testament we read, "The zeal of the LORD of hosts will do this." The Bible describes Jesus as zealous. Isaiah 59:17 prophesied about Him this way, "For he put on righteousness as a breastplate, and an helmet of salvation upon his head; and he put on the garments of vengeance for clothing, and was clad with zeal as a cloak."

The disciples understood that Psalms 69:9 spoke of Him this way, "For the zeal of thine house hath eaten me up; and the reproaches of them that reproached thee are fallen upon me."

Jesus' passion was His Father's will. He said in John 4:34, "Jesus saith unto them, 'My meat is to do the will of him that sent me, and to finish his work.'"

## Our zeal for God should burn hot within us

The Bible also encourages believers to pursue a passionate or zealous personal relationship with God.

- Prov. 13:4: The soul of the sluggard desireth, and hath nothing: but the soul of the diligent shall be made fat.
- Eccl. 9:10: Whatsoever thy hand finds to do, do it with thy might; for there is no work, nor device, nor knowledge, nor wisdom, in the grave, whither thou goest.
- Gal. 4:18: But it is good to be zealously affected always in a good thing, and not only when I am present with you.
- 1 Cor. 14:12: Even so ye, forasmuch as ye are zealous of spiritual gifts, seek that ye may excel to the edifying of the church.
- Paul speaks of his own passion in Colossians 1:29: "Whereunto I also labour, striving according to his working, which worketh in me mightily."
- Titus 2:14 describes Jesus this way: "Who gave himself for us, that he might redeem us from all iniquity, and purify unto himself a peculiar people, zealous of good works.
- Paul said to Timothy in 2 Timothy 1:6, "Wherefore I put thee in remembrance

that thou stir up the gift of God, which is in thee by the putting on of my hands."

> David, said, "My zeal for God and his work burns hot within me." (Ps. 69:9 LB)

John Wesley was once asked why so many people came to hear him preach. He said, "I just set myself on fire and the people come to watch me burn!" Are we 'on fire' for God? These are good examples of godly passions. Tommy Tenney made this statement:

> I used to pursue preaching good sermons and great crowds, and attempt great accomplishments for Him. But I've been ruined. Now I'm a God chaser. Nothing else matters anymore. I tell you that as your brother in Christ, I love you. But I love Him more. I couldn't care less about what other people or ministers think about me. I'm going after God. That's not a pride thing; it's a hunger thing. When you pursue God with all your heart, soul, and body,

He will turn to meet you and you will come out of it ruined for the world.
- Tommy Tenney, *The God Chasers: Pursuing the Lover of Your Soul*

As a young man in theological seminary my heart burned for missions. I dreamed of serving God oversees in a missionary context. Thoughts of teaching, training, planting churches, reaching unreached people groups, and crossing cultural barriers with the gospel occupied my every waking thought. I read books, travelled to countries with a high percentage of unreached people, spoke to missionaries, attended conferences, studied about unreached people groups; it was just bursting in my heart. As you can probably imagine it wasn't long before my family and I were serving as missionaries in Ghana where we worked for over a decade. God gives us different passions so everything He wants done in the world will get done.

## 7 Keys to Igniting your Passion

### 1. Share your purpose

You may know your purpose but you lack passion. One of the ways to ignite your passion is to share what God has called you to do with other likeminded people. Be sure that you're sharing something that matters. It's difficult to get excited about something that doesn't matter to us. One of my passions was to plant a church in Virginia. During the early stages of the church plant I shared my passion with friends, colleagues and everyone who would listen. It was partly my infectious passion that compelled a number of people to support us in prayer, as well as emotional and financial support.

### 2. Pursue a dream.

One of the greatest obstacles for people pursuing their dreams is the fear of failure. Before they even try, they've already determined that the odds are stacked against them so much that they might as well not start. I certainly understand the difficulties in achieving many dreams. At time the chances of success are so overwhelmingly against us that we have a better chance of getting hit by lightning on a clear day. But hyperboles aside, the big question remains. Why would someone pursue a dream when the odds are stacked against them? The answer is that it's the pursuit of dream that will ignite our passion and our passion is the compass, propelling us toward our purpose, fulfilling our incredible destiny.

*3. Fight an enemy.*

This might sound strange, but nonetheless it's very true. It was David's passion for God and love for God's people that led him to the valley of Sochoh where Goliath was breathing out threats against the God of Israel and the people of God. (See 1 Samuel 17.) It was his passion first and foremost for Yahweh that gave him the courage to confront this nine-foot giant. So ask yourself this question: What do you hate? What do you wish you could change? Is there something that is beckoning you from the stands to the playing field? It may well be your passion stirring within you. Listen to it; respond to it because it's carrying your potential and your purpose.

*4. Look for the good*

As you go about your job or your studies, look for certain aspects you enjoy. If you keep a journal, write down at least one specific instance each day about a part of your studies that you found fulfilling, challenging, or just plain fun. When you put in the extra effort to look for things that bring you joy, no matter how small you'll find your attitude changing, sending you in the direction of your destiny.

*5. Stop complaining*

Just as looking for things we love, will help us grow our passion, while complaining will stifle and even kill it. Even if we have valid reasons to be frustrated, we must be aware that complaining will never improve our situation. Rather we must choose to wait to mention the problem until we can offer a solution. Until then, we mustn't allow our minds to dwell on the negatives. Philippians 2: 4 says, "Do all things without grumbling or questioning."

*6. Rest*

When we're sleep deprived, we will always be more easily frustrated and confused – two key factors that lead to a lack of passion. As we connect with your passion in pursuit of our purpose, we must choose to spend time resting in God's presence. In this instance I refer to physical rest and sleep.

> And he said to them, "Come away by yourselves to a desolate place and rest a while." For many were coming and going, and they had no leisure even to eat. (Mark 6:31)

Also the Psalmist says,

> It is in vain that you rise up early and go late to rest, eating the bread of anxious toil; for he gives to his beloved sleep. (Ps. 127:2)

To become passionate requires a certain amount of energy so be sure to take time the time you need to rest.


## 7. Delight in the Lord

Prayer connects us with the One from whom all passion and purpose originates. If we're becoming passionate about prayer and connecting with

God we know our passion is being stirred up. It's during moments of prayer, worship and meditation that God will inspire us with desires that are dear to His heart.

The psalmist says:

> Take delight in the Lord, and He will give you the desires of your heart. (Ps. 37:4)

As we take delight in the Lord our hearts find deep peace and fulfillment in Him.  If we truly find satisfaction and worth in Christ, Scripture says He will give us the longings of our hearts. Does that mean, if we go to church every Sunday, God will give us a new Rolls Royce? No. The idea behind this verse and others like it is that, when we truly rejoice or "delight" in the eternal things of God, our desires will begin to parallel His and we will never lack what we need. Matthew 6:33 says this: "But seek first his kingdom and his righteousness, and all these things [the necessities of life] will be given to you as well." That includes our passion and ultimately our purpose.

# Chapter 8

## IT'S TIME TO MAKE YOUR MOVE

### Joshua 1: 1-2

*Now after the death of Moses the servant of the LORD it came to pass, that the **LORD** spoke unto **Joshua** the son of Nun, Moses' minister, saying, **Moses my servant is dead; NOW** therefore arise, go over this Jordan, you, and all this people, unto the land which I do give to them, even to the children of Israel.*

The Book of Joshua marks the fulfillment of God's ancient promise to the children of Israel, namely that they would inherit a land given to them by God. I like this book because it marks an end of one era, a new beginning and the emergence of a new generation. The focus is a young, up-and-coming Hebrew leader by the name of Joshua. The name Joshua is a rendering of the Hebrew word "Yehoshua", meaning "Yahweh is salvation." The first five books of the Bible, commonly referred to as the Pentateuch, cover the early history of the world and include the origin and development of the nation of Israel up till the time of its entry into the Promised Land. It goes on to describe the details of this incredible exploit. The Book of Joshua is also a metaphor for people who are trapped in the wilderness of life and long for their own crossing into purpose and meaning. As the book opens we see Joshua grieving the loss of an old friend and mentor. It was a time of mourning and the sound of lament could be heard coming from every tent in the camp of Israel. The news of Moses' death was unbearable. It begins:

> After the death of Moses the servant of the Lord, it came to pass that the Lord spoke to Joshua the son of Nunn. (Josh. 1:1)

In this case 'after' is an adjective that describes a process, course of action, development or progression. Up until this point, Joshua's purpose as a leader was not fully realized. Even though the death of Moses was a great loss to him and his generation it was necessary to bring out the greatness that was within Joshua. The loss of a great friend and mentor was a part of the process toward his greatness. Remember Joshua was among the people who had left Egypt forty years earlier. He had seen a whole generation die and be buried in sandy graves along the route to Canaan. They died en route to their destiny. Many of us like the idea of the promise but aren't that excited about the process. Yet without the process the promise has no personal value. In the same way, everything you've been through up until this point is part and parcel of your climb toward greatness.

Make no mistake the death of Moses was a tragedy on a number of fronts. Not only did they lose a great and godly leader, but the death of Moses would have meant that Israel was vulnerable to surrounding enemies. This was a crisis by any stretch of the imagination. Yet quite often God uses such moments of crisis to launch us into purpose. This crisis could include divorce, loss of a loved one, sickness, raising children with

Down-syndrome or some kind of personal failure. Joshua was in mourning but the show had to go on.

**MOSES...** *my servant is* ***DEAD!*** (Josh. 1:1)

Imagine the shock! How could Moses be dead? Moses was the one who spoke to God like a man speaks to his friends. Moses was the one who had the courage to confront Pharaoh and led the exodus out of Egypt. It was Moses who lifted up his rod, parting the Red Sea. Moses was the one who changed God's mind when He decided to wipe out the nation of Israel for their idolatry. It was Moses' reputation as a leader that kept their enemies at bay. But often we find that the purpose of God is revealed in the crucible of tragedy and loss. Some things have to die before we can enter into our promise land of purpose. Moses was dead but a new season was born in the life of the nation.

> *Moses my servant is* ***DEAD.***" **NOW!!!** Timing is important–now is the time to move.

As long as Moses was alive it was not Joshua's time to step out.

"Moses my servant is dead. Now then, you and all these people, get ready to cross the Jordan into the land I am about to give them..." (Josh. 1: 2)

In effect, God was saying, "Turn the page, Joshua. Moses was a great man, he was my servant, but he's gone. It's time for you to move on." For those of us who are still in the desert, God is saying: "Turn the page. Let go of the past. It's time to move on." The greatest obstacle to living out your purpose is your refusal to let go of yesterday.

## TWO THINGS THAT ARE NEEDED TO "MAKE YOUR MOVE"

### 1. First and foremost we have to be God's own.

*God encouraged Joshua* - In the first chapter God realizes that Joshua lacks courage and he tells him five times to be courageous. Over and over God told Joshua that He was with him just like He was with Moses. Just like Moses and other leaders that would come later, Joshua had to be God's man above all else. Only God's men and woman can speak with a prophetic voice without fear of reprisal or human consequence. Only when we can resolve in the words of the old song: "Take the whole world but give me Jesus." Only when you *"love not the World neither the things in the world* can you earn God's trust. As you make your move into living a purpose-driven life remember that above all else you belong to God.

### 2. *You have to be Courageous*

Joshua was told repeatedly:

- "Be strong and courageous, because you will lead these people to inherit the land I swore to their ancestors to give them. Be strong and very courageous."
- "Have I not commanded you? Be strong and courageous."
- "Do not be afraid; do not be discouraged, for the LORD your God will be with you wherever you go."
- "Only be strong and courageous!"

The reason God went to such great lengths to infuse courage into Joshua's heart was because a leader without courage is easily taken influenced by popular opinion and the powers that be. Like Joshua we too must have courage if we are to fulfill our life's purpose. Courage—which is bravery, boldness, and fearlessness—is the ability to confront fear, pain, danger, uncertainty, or intimidation. Ernest Hemingway famously defined courage as 'grace under pressure'.

According to Maya Angelou:

> Courage is the most important of the virtues, because without courage you can't practice any other virtue consistently. You can practice any virtue erratically, but nothing consistently without courage.

Or this insight from Winston Churchill,

> Courage is rightly esteemed the first of human qualities because it is the quality that guarantees all others.

In medieval virtue ethics, championed by Averroes and Thomas Aquinas and still important in Roman Catholic circles, courage is referred to as

"Fortitude." It is one of the four cardinal virtues, along with prudence, justice, and temperance. According to Cornel West, to have courage is to look unflinchingly into catastrophic circumstances and muster the will to overcome the fear or threat it presents. Probably the single greatest hindrance to fulfillment of destiny is a lack of courage. Like Joshua standing at the dawn of a new age and the new generations of Israelites longing for the Promised Land, it's time to make your move. This is our season and the time to grasp hold of our purpose and refuse to let it go.

It's amazing what can be achieved with resolve. Look at Joshua:

> *Then Joshua commanded the officers of the people, saying, pass through the camp and command the people, saying: Prepare provisions for yourselves, for **within three days** you will cross over this Jordan, to go into possess the land which the Lords your God is giving you to possess.* (Josh 1:10)

At this point we see Joshua who had always stood in Moses' shadow. Now we see a man stepping into his purpose, instructing, commanding and taking hold of the vision. Here we see Joshua with a definite purpose, a purpose that Moses couldn't have carried out. One man completes the work of another. Moses was a legislator while Joshua was a soldier. Joshua was a man who saw only the purpose and heard only the command, who had no ear for objection, but a great capacity for inspiration. People who walk in their purpose are doers and not just thinkers. The secret to life is not thought but action and Joshua was a man of action.

If we're going to fulfill our God-given purpose we're going to have to act even we take baby steps. Write down an action plan, arrange to speak to a mentor, carry out a feasibility study, conduct as spiritual gift assessment or arrange to volunteer – just make a move in your area of gifting and calling.

**Stepping into Purpose**

I will close out this book by leaving you with

five things that the children of Israel had to do
before they entered their Promised Land and
what we must do to enter into our God-given
purpose.

## 1.  They had to cross their own Jordan

Joshua 3:17

> Meanwhile, the priests who were carrying
> the Ark of the LORD's Covenant stood on
> dry ground in the middle of the riverbed
> as the people passed by. They waited there
> until the whole nation of Israel had
> crossed the Jordan on dry ground.

The generation that crossed the Red Sea under
Moses had all but died off leaving just Joshua
and Caleb. If this new Joshua generation was going to enter into the Promised Land they would
have to have their own testimony and experience

of crossing over. Every one of us who live according to purpose will at some point, have to face our Red Sea moment. It is at that moment when we must take that leap of faith to follow our passion and purpose. Perhaps we've been working a job we hate but stay with it because it pays the bills and then we decide to resign and pursue our passions. It could be that moment when we launch our own ministry or business. The crossing moment is that split-second when we make up our minds to bring everything we do in line with our purpose. When that happens, it's the greatest feeling ever.

## 2. Remember what the Lord has brought you out of

Joshua 4:1

> Each of you is to take up a stone on his shoulder, according to the number of the tribes of the Israelites, to serve as a sign among you. In the future, when your children ask you, 'What do these stones mean?' tell them that the flow of the Jordan was cut off before the ark of the covenant of the Lord. When it crossed the Jordan, the waters of

> the Jordan were cut off. These stones are to be a memorial to the people of Israel forever.

Once you've crossed over into purpose and you're living your dream remember that it was the Lord who brought you out. Once we hit that sweet spot and things are just flowing and flourishing do not forget to be thankful. Keep a token to remind where you came from and to remind you of God's faithfulness.

### 3. Take a sharp knife
Joshua 5:2

> At that time the LORD told Joshua, "Make flint knives and circumcise this second generation of Israelites."

The Joshua generation was never circumcised but God tolerated it because they were in the wilderness. However, once they were ready to cross over into the Promised Land they had to leave the excess foreskin behind. In the same way, when we make up our minds to live out our purpose there are some things we cannot take with us. This could include certain friends, mindsets, attitudes, behaviors, spiritual immaturity, and so on. Just as God told Joshua to take a sharp knife and circumcise every male, we too have to cut away and leave behind things that work against our purpose.

### 4. The Manna ceased
Joshua 5:12

> The manna stopped the day after they ate this food from the land; there was no longer any manna for the Israelites, but that year they ate of the produce of Canaan.

For forty years God provided manna for the children of Israel while they wandered in the wilderness. They did not sow or harvest their own crop but God miraculously provided for them as if they were helpless babes. Then when they were about to enter the Promised Land something incredible happened: the manna ceased! They were now to eat the fruit they harvested with their own hands. The point here is that we cannot maintain a diet of aimlessness once we step into purpose. What we read, watch, hear, practice and believe must line up with our purpose so that we're moving and active and not simply a bystander watching the action. The right kinds of food are also essential for growth and development of our purpose.

### 5. Confront Jericho
Joshua 6: 1-2

> Now Jericho was securely shut up because of the children of Israel; none went out, and none came in. And the Lord said to Joshua: "See! I have given Jericho into your hand, its king, and the mighty men of valor."

It must have come as a quite shock when Joshua raced toward Jericho to be met with a towering wall and fortified gates. Listen to what the Lord said to Joshua, "See! I have given Jericho into your hand…" Every person who lives a life of purpose must have a vision of success that is more real than any physical reality. In other words God was saying that His word, which declared that the land was theirs, was a more powerful reality than the physical wall and armed

warriors defending the fortress. Practice visual-
izing yourself living out your purpose and finding your place of significance. Meditate on your
purpose, see yourself swimming in it and speak
it forth. Romans for 4:17:

> As it is written, I have made you the father
> of many nations. [He was appointed our
> father] in the sight of God in Whom he be-
> lieved, Who gives life to the dead and
> speaks of the nonexistent things that [He
> has foretold and promised] as if they [al-
> ready] existed.

# POSTSCRIPT

I pray that these pages have been of help to you on your journey to finding your unique significance. One key aspect of the lessons taught in these pages is the importance of God being the architect of our purpose and destiny. We have discussed time and again in this book the necessity of having a personal relationship with God through Jesus Christ, as the starting point of discovering your life's meaning. If you are not in relationship with Jesus, I would like to offer the opportunity for you to surrender your life to Him today. It's easy, just say this simply prayer:

*Lord Jesus, I realize you are the creator and*
*sustainer of my life,*
*I want to know you not only as my creator but*
*as my Savor and Lord.*

*Please forgive me of my past sins and wrongs*
*and come into my heart.*
*Lord Jesus, I surrender my life to you today and*
*ask you to guide me into my true purpose and*
*reason for being born into this world.*
*Amen*

Now go and unleash your God-given purpose
and make your mark on the world.